First Printing, 2020

Just B Cause Books

hollowaycecelia@sbcglobal.net
www.justbcause.org

GOD's RAINBOW PEOPLE

by Cecelia F. Holloway

Illustrated by Chris House

DEDICATION

This book is dedicated to children all over the world. The origin of this story was taken from what many consider to be the greatest book ever written, the Holy Bible.

I wrote this to help children understand the unique differences of all people—language, background, likes and dislikes—which fit into the divine plan of God. Regardless of our differences none of us is a mistake, an accident or cursed in any way. The great variety in physical appearance, speech, culture, family traits, skills and abilities were all designed by God, making every single person a one-of-a-kind original creation.

As you read this book to children, let them know we are all an important part of an amazing rainbow of colors, languages, skills and abilities.

God's plan for every one of us is so specific, down to the smallest detail—when and where we were born, unique cultures and experiences, our family members, our skin tone, hair, facial features and body type—all working together, to create billions of special people.

God doesn't make mistakes. He created an amazing world for us, and we are all part of His beautiful plan to have a 'Rainbow of People'.

POEM

God's Rainbow of People

Written by Cecelia Holloway

What a wonderful, beautiful sight God must see

When He looks down at His Rainbow of People

He'll see you, and you, and me!

A beautiful bouquet of colors
Different heights, shapes and sizes
Different languages and cultures
He'll see different skills, different gifts
and different abilities

I believe it puts a smile on God's face
When He looks at what we call the human race

Don't change yourself to look like me
Let's embrace our differences and
Live in peace and harmony

That's the way God wanted it to be!

In the beginning God created the heavens and the earth. He filled the earth with all kinds of animals, in many different shapes, sizes, and colors.

He also created flowers and plants of many shapes and sizes. They were all different and very beautiful.

One day, God created a man named Adam and gave him a wife named Eve. He told them to have lots of children and fill the earth with people.
So they did.

Soon, many people lived on earth just like God wanted, but there was a problem. They were too much alike! They all looked, talked, dressed and lived the same way.

One day the people decided to build a super tall tower so they could go up to heaven. God wanted the people to stay on earth since He created the earth and filled it with beautiful plants and animals for them to enjoy.

God thought to himself, "I've made all the flowers and plants many different colors. All the animals are different colors too. Everything on earth is different and beautiful, except for my people."

So, God changed their language, making them all speak differently, and they couldn't understand each other anymore.

God didn't want everyone to look, talk or behave the same. He wanted them to be different. After He changed their language, God made the people spread out all over the world.

Some people moved to warm places while others went to very cold places. Over time their way of living and skin color also changed.
All around the world people became very different from each other, just the way God wanted.

Those changes happened many, many years ago, and their differences made God happy because they became a rainbow of people. They were finally unique, just like the plants and animals on earth. All around the world people spoke different languages and had different ways to live, work, play, eat, and sleep.

Because of the changes God made, people today are all different colors, sizes, and shapes. They have different faces, eyes, ears, mouths and noses.

You are an important part of God's rainbow of people. Be proud of how special and unique you are. Love the differences you see in other people because they are special too.

**Draw a picture of
YOURSELF!**

We are all part of
GOD'S RAINBOW PEOPLE!